Bruges Flower Lace Patterns

EDNA SUTTON

Abbreviations
cl st   cloth stitch
h st   half stitch
d st   double stitch
b st   back stitch

No. 1   Mobile or coaster

Thread Belgian No. 60/2 linen

Techniques
Flower No. 5, cl st, h st, d st, plait-with-picot, false plait, d st edge braid, sewings, Edging No. 1

Order of work
1) Flower No. 5
2) Outer d st edge braid and false plaits
3) Edging No. 1
double stitch

No. 2   Decoration for a child's dress

Thread Belgian No. 60/2 linen

Techniques
Cl st, h st, d st, b st, sewings, d st edge braid, scrolls, plait-with-picot, tally

Order of work
1) Scroll, d st edge braid, scroll
2) Half circle braid
3) Three petals (h st or cl st), plait-with-picot filling, worked as the petal progresses. Plait-with-picots to join to the scrolls

---

No. 3   Motif for serviette or tablecloth

Thread Belgian No. 60/2 linen

Techniques
Cl st, h st, d st, b st, flower No. 1, picots, d st edge braid, sewings, scrolls, edging No. 1, hanging in and throwing out pairs, false plait, setting up as for a leaf

Order of work
1) Central d st edge braid, hanging on and throwing out as for a leaf
2) Flower No. 1, using the braid to set up and sew out the pairs
3) Scroll, d st edge braid, scroll

1

No. 4 Edging for table linen

Thread As for No. 3

Techniques
As for No. 3

Order of work
Work as for No. 3, using a sewing and a false plait to join the motifs together

No. 5 Corner for table linen

Thread As for No. 3

Techniques
As for No. 3

Order of work
Work as for No. 3, using a continuous braid at the curve, working the Dieppe ground filling between the two braids

No. 6 Motif for a skirt or apron

Thread Belgian No. 60/2 linen

Techniques
Cl st, h st, d st, b st, d st edge braid, scrolls, sewings, leaf with h st vein, edging No. 1, flower No. 5

Order of work
1) Scroll, d st edge braid, scroll. Do not forget the false plait
2) Flower No. 5, taking care to sew in the pairs accurately and sew them out carefully
3) Leaf, h st vein braid, simple d st edge braid, the h st vein braid and the leaf. Do not forget the plait-with-picot join

No. 7 Motif for a work bag

Thread Belgian No. 60/2 linen

Techniques
Cl st, h st, d st, b st, false plaits, sewings, d st edge braid, flower No. 3, filling No. 3, filling No. 5, picots, plait-with-picot

Order of work
1) Flower No. 3
2) Scrolls and Central braids and the small areas of filling
3) Outer d st edge braid, scrolls, false plaits, sewings, to join to the centre motif
4) Small braid, scrolls, filling
5) Filling No. 5

No. 8   Bell pull

Thread Belgian No. 60/2 linen

Techniques
Cl st, h st, d st, d st edge braid, false plait, filling No. 3, filling No. 1, filling
No. 5, filling No. 6, filling No. 7, filling No. 4

Order of work
1) Scroll, d st edge braid, scroll
2) Fillings

No. 9   Handkerchief

Thread Belgian No. 120/2 linen

Techniques
Cl st, h st, d st, d st edge braid, scrolls, sewing into the edge of the braid,
filling No. 3, edging No. 1, plait with picot, sewings

Order of work
1) Flower No. 5
2) Scrolls and braid
3) Filling No. 4
4) D st edge braid
5) Edging No. 1

No. 10   Doily

Thread Belgian No. 60/2 linen

Techniques
Cl st, h st, d st, d st edge braid, flower No. 2, filling No. 1, filling No. 3,
shaped d st edge braid worked alternatively in cl st and h st, sewings,
raised edge, plait-with-picot

Order of work
1) Flower No. 2
2) D st edge braids and the small areas of filling No. 3
3) Filling No. 1
4) End braids, worked as a raised edge
5) Shaped braids

No. 11   Tray, motif mounted under glass

Thread Belgian No. 60/2 linen

Techniques
Cl st, h st, d st, plaits, tally, flower No. 7, filling No. 1, filling No. 3, filling
No. 5, crossing of braids, leaves with 'ladder' or h st vein, d st edge braid,
edging No. 1, plait-with-picot

Order of work
1) Flower No. 7
2) Leaves
3) Scroll, braid, scroll and small areas of filling No. 3
4) Filling No. 1
5) Filling No. 5
6) Edging No. 1

No. 12 Lampshade panels

Thread Belgian No. 60/2 linen

Techniques
Cl st, h st, d st, plait-with-picot, flower No. 6, d st edge braid, scrolls, raised edge in centre of leaf

Order of work
1) Flower No. 6
2) Scroll and braid
3) Braid and leaves, working the plait-with-picot joins

No. 13 Doily

Thread Belgian No. 60/2 linen

Techniques
Cl st, h st, d st, curved d st edge braid with cl st, and h st sections, leaves, b st, false plaits, flower No. 5, sewings, filling No. 5

Order of work
1) Flower No. 5
2) Outer braid
3) Leaves and filling No. 3

No. 14 Coffee cloth (linen fabric centre)

Thread Belgian No. 60/2 linen

Techniques
Cl st, h st, d st, b st, scrolls, d st edge braid, h st vein, ladder vein, flower No. 3, false plaits, filling No. 3, plait-with-picot, raised edge

Order of work
1) The inner braid, wide sections in cl st, divided with a row of d st, shown by the arrow
2) Flower No. 3
3) Scrolls and braids, working the plaits-with-picots, false plaits and sewings
4) Leaf shapes, with a central raised edge, and plait-with-picot
5) Outer scrolls and braid, with a h st vein. Sections are divided with a row of d st. False plaits and plait-with-picot

No. 15 Fan

Thread DMC Retors D'Alsace No. 30

Techniques
Cl st, h st, d st, b st, d st edge braid, straight edge (raised edge), raised edge, curved edge braid, worked alternately in cl st and h st, flower No. 1, scrolls, filling No. 3, filling No. 5, false plaits, Dieppe ground

Order of work
1) Flower No. 1
2) Scrolls and d st edge braid, plaits-with-picots
3) Centre and end motifs
4) Narrow braid, d st edge braid at the sides. Inner braid and straight edge braid at the top (raised edge), false plaits to join to the motifs
5) Fillings No. 3 and 5
6) Curved braid, Cl st and h st sections separated with a row of d st

No. 16 Coffee cloth

Thread Belgian No. 60/2 linen

Techniques
Cl st, h st, d st, b st, flower No. 5, scrolls, d st edge braid, false plait, filling
No. 3, filling No. 2, sewings, plait-with-picot, edging No. 1

Order of work
1) Work all the flowers
2) Inner scrolls and braids, small areas of filling No. 2 and false plaits
3) Filling No. 2
4) Outer scrolls and braids, sewings
5) Large areas of filling No. 3
6) Edging No. 1

No. 17 Large doily

Thread Belgian No. 60/2 linen

Techniques
Cl st, h st, d st, b st, flower No. 5, the Lily, d st edge braid, edging No. 1,
sewings, plait-with-picot, raised edge, filling No. 1, filling No. 3

Order of work
1) Centre circle
2) Flowers
3) Lilies and small areas of filling No. 3
4) Filling No. 1
5) D st edge braid
6) Large areas of filling No. 3
7) Edging No. 1

No. 18 Large doily

Thread Belgian No. 60/2 linen

Techniques
Cl st, h st, d st, b st, shaped d st edge braid with cl st and h st sections,
sewings, flower No. 5, plait-with-picot, shaped petal worked in cl st and h
st sections separated with a row of d st, filling No. 3, edging No. 1

Order of work
1) Flower No. 5
2) Shaped petals and plaits-with-picots
3) Shaped d st edge braid, sewings made into the shaped petals
4) Edging No. 1

No. 19 Doily

Thread Belgian No. 60/2 linen

Techniques
Cl st, h st, d st, b st, d st edge braid, shaped braid, h st vein braid, scrolls,
false plait, plait-with-picot, sewings, filling No. 5

Order of work
1) Work all the flowers and centre motif
2) Scrolls, h st vein braid, shaped braid, false plaits, small areas of plait-
with-picot filling
3) Filling No. 5

No. 20 Coffee cloth

Thread Belgian No. 60/2 linen

Techniques
Cl st, h st, d st, b st, d st edge braid, flower No. 6, filling No. 3, filling No. 6, edging No. 3 (variation), false plait, plait-with-picot

Order of work
1) Centre flower
2) Centre braid
3) 'Half flowers', attached to the centre braid, plait-with-picot
4) Filling No. 6
5) Outer braid
6) Filling No. 3
7) Edging No. 3

No. 21 Tray cloth

Thread Belgian No. 60/2 linen

Techniques
Cl st, h st, d st, b st, d st edge braid, scrolls, crossing of braids, leaves with h st vein, filling No. 3, filling No. 5, false plaits, sewings, plaits

Order of work
1) Centre circle and filling
2) Flowers
3) Centre leaves and filling No. 3
4) Outer braid, scrolls, loops and crossing of braids
5) Leaves attached to the outer braid
6) Filling No. 5, filling No. 3

No. 22 Large centre piece

Thread Belgian No. 60/2 linen

Techniques
Cl st, h st, d st, b st, d st edge braid, crossing of braids, tally, plait-with-picot, lily, flower No. 7, plait, leaves, sewings, false plaits, filling No. 3, filling No. 5, edging No. 1 (variation)

Order of work
1) Centre circle
2) Centre flowers, braid and leaves
3) The lilies
4) Outer braid and small areas of filling
5) Filling No. 5
6) Filling No. 3
7) Outer flowers
8) Outer circles and plait-with-picot joins
9) Outer edge braid and plait-with-picot joins
10) Edging No. 1 (variation)

No. 23 Collar

Thread Tanne No. 30 or DMC Retors D'Alsace No. 30

Techniques
Cl st, h st, d st, b st, d st edge braid, crossing of braids, scrolls, tally, straight edge (raised edge), filling No. 2, filling No. 5, flowers No. 7, sewings, edging No. 1, false plait

Order of work
1) Neck edge braid
2) Flowers and tallies
3) Outer braids, scrolls, crossing of braids, false plaits and tallies
4) Filling No. 2
5) Filling No. 5
6) Edging No. 1

No. 24 Large centre piece

Thread Belgian No. 60/2 linen

Techniques
Cl st, h st, d st, b st, d st edge braid, h st vein braid, shaped braid divided with plaits, flower No. 10, filling No. 3, false plaits, crossing of braids, sewings, tally, leaf (raised centre edge)

Order of work
1) Centre flower
2) Inner braid, h st vein, shaped braid, sections divided with plaits, plait-with-picot joins, false plaits
3) Filling No. 1
4) Flowers, plait-with-picot joins, false plaits
5) Outer braid, h st vein braid, crossing of braids, small areas of filling No. 3, plait-with-picot joins, fillings within the loops of braid
6) Tallies

Suppliers

Alby Lace Centre
Cromer Road
Alby
Norwich
Norfolk

Frank Herring & Sons
27 High West Street
Dorchester
DT1 1UP

Loricraft
4 Big Lane
Lambourn
Berks RG16 7XQ

Honiton Lace Shop
44 High Street
Honiton
Devon

Mace and Nairn
89 Crane Street
Salisbury
Wilts

The Lace Guild
The Hollies
53 Audnam
Stourbridge
West Midlands
DY8 4AE

D.H. Shaw
47 Zamor Crescent
Thurscroft
Rotherham
South Yorks

John & Jennifer Ford

October Hill
Upper Way
Upper Longdon
Rugeley
Staffs WS15 1QB

Shireburn Lace
Finkle Court
Finkle
Serburn in Elmet
North Yorks

Enid Taylor
Valley House Craft Studio
Ruston
Scarborough
North Yorks
YO13 9QE

George White
Delaheys Cottage
Thistle Hill
Knaresborough
North Yorks

English Lace School
Oak House
Church Stile
Woodbury
near Exeter
Devon

D.J. Hornsby
149 High Street
Burton Latimer
Kettering
Northants
NN15 5RL

Capt J.R. Howell
19 Summerwood Lane

Halsall
nr Ormskirk
Lancs
L39 8RG

Sebalace
Waterloo Mill
Howden Road
Silsden
West Yorks BD20 0HA

T. Brown
Woodside
Greenlands Lane
Prestwood
Great Missenden
Bucks

A. Sells
49 Pedley Lane
Clifton
Shefford
Beds

C. & D. Springett
21 Hillmorton Road
Rugby
Warks CV22 5DF

B. Phillips
Pantaglas
Cellen
Lampeter
Dyfed

Newnham Lace
    Equipment
11 Dorchester Close
Basingstoke
Hants RG23 8EX

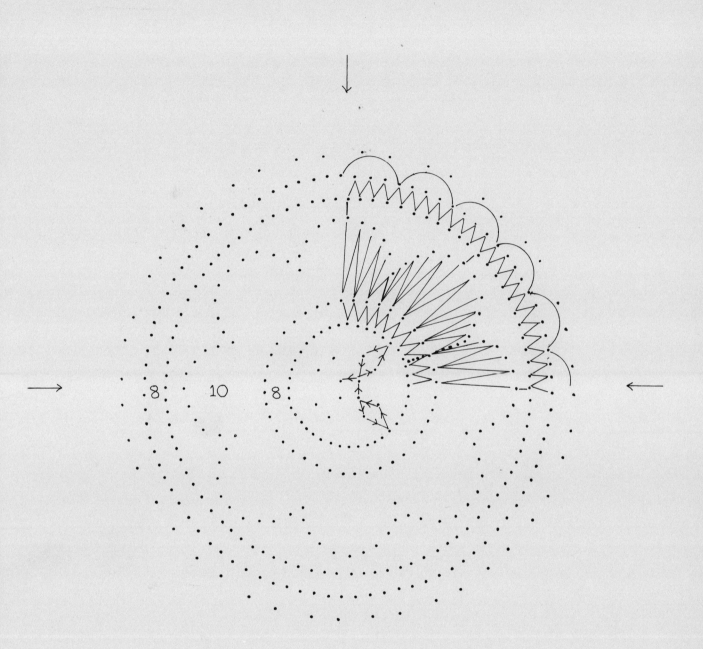

8   10   8

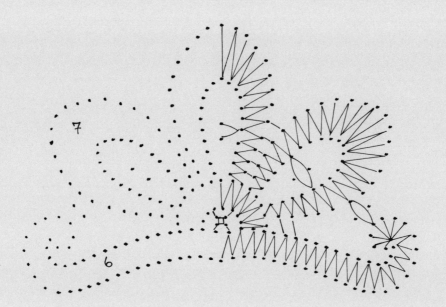

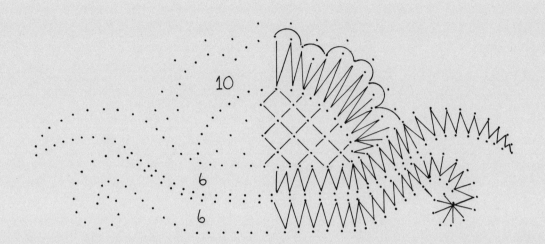

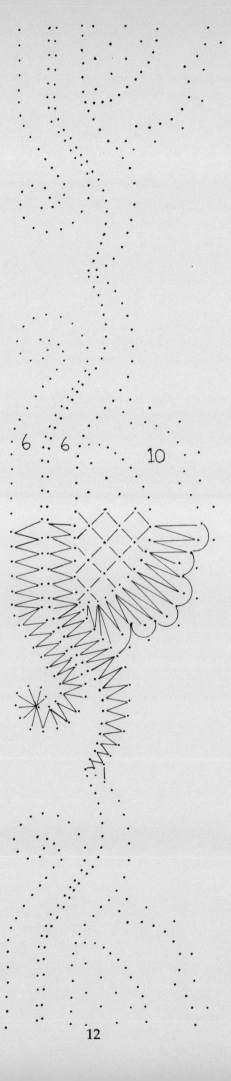

6 6   10

Inner
Edge

6   6   10

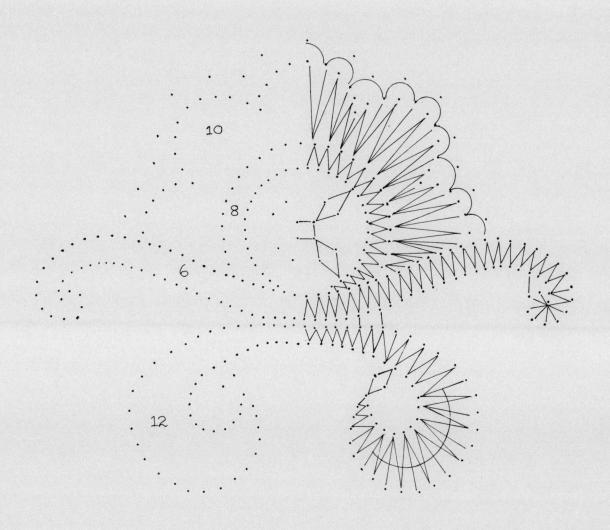

10

8

6

12

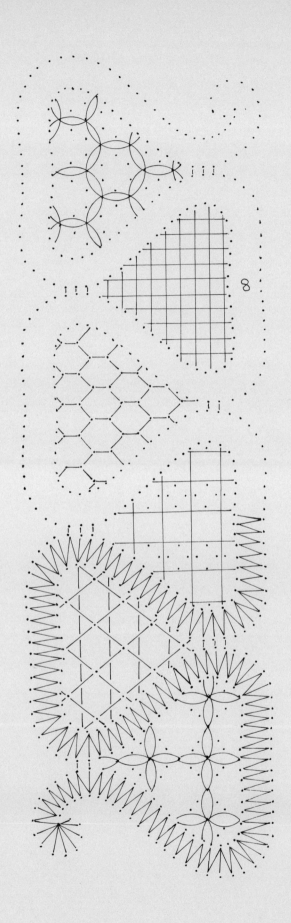

Start here

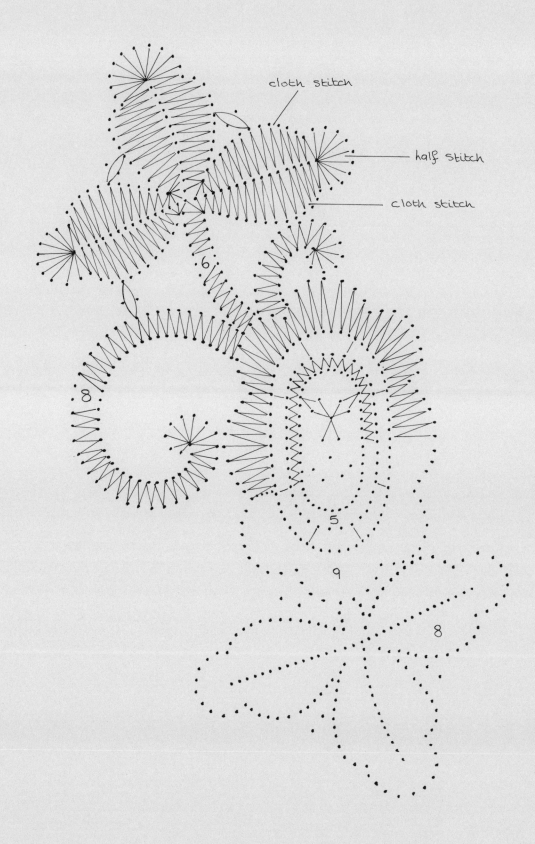

cloth stitch

half stitch

cloth stitch

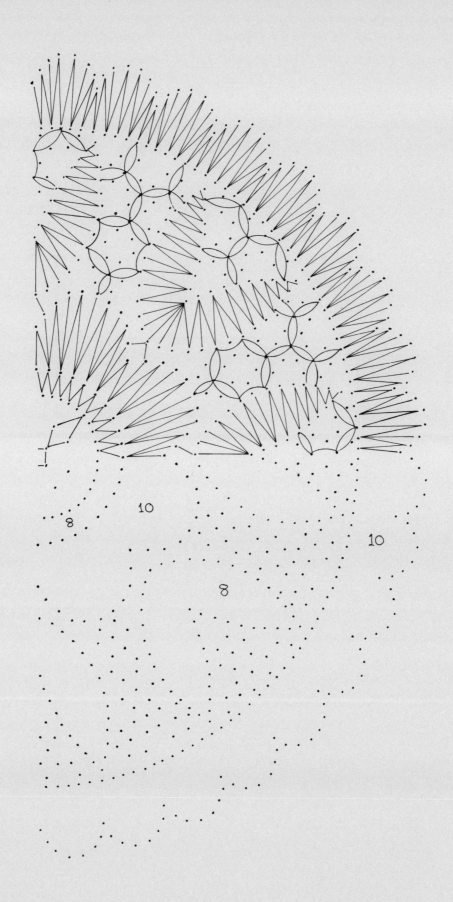

8

10

10

8

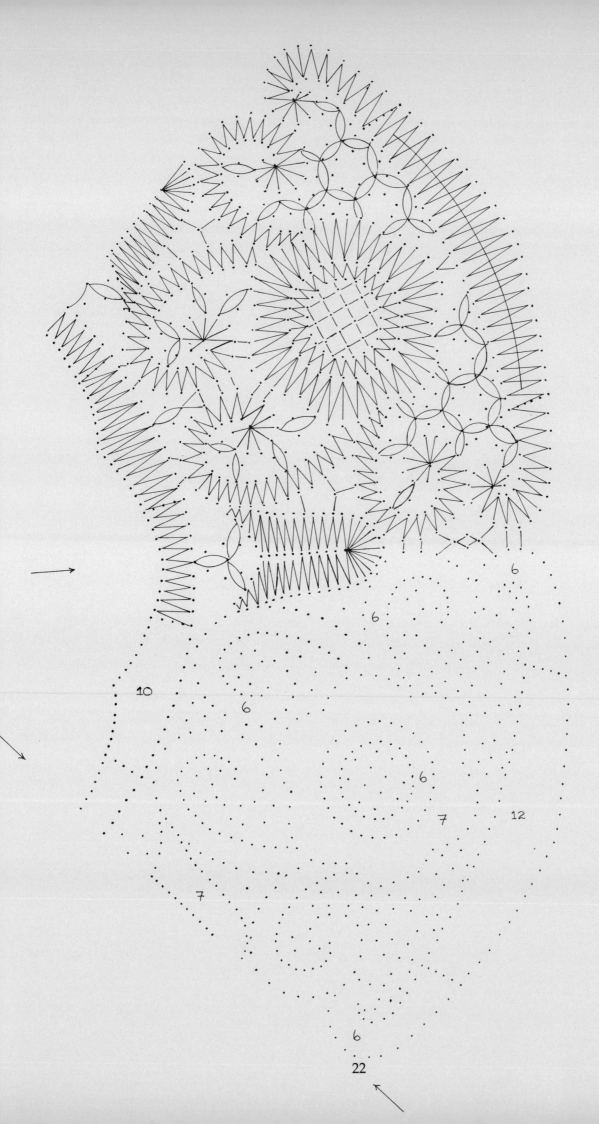

14

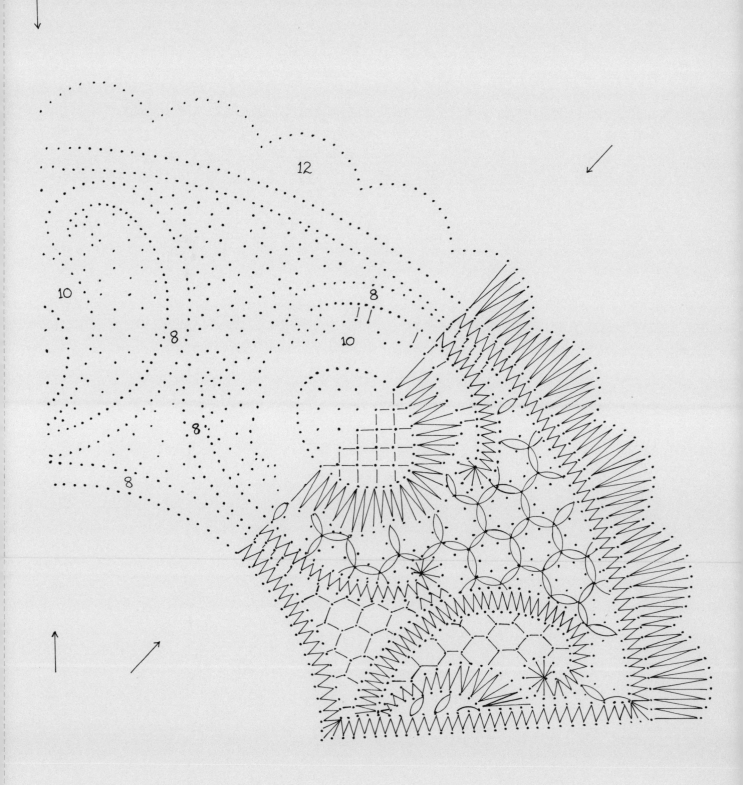

12

10

8

8

10

8

8

8

8

10

8

25

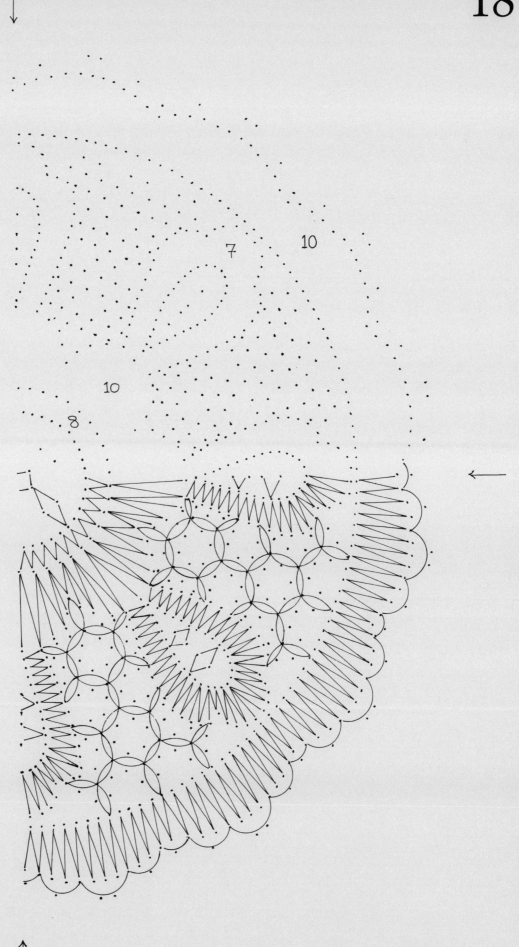

7

10

10

8

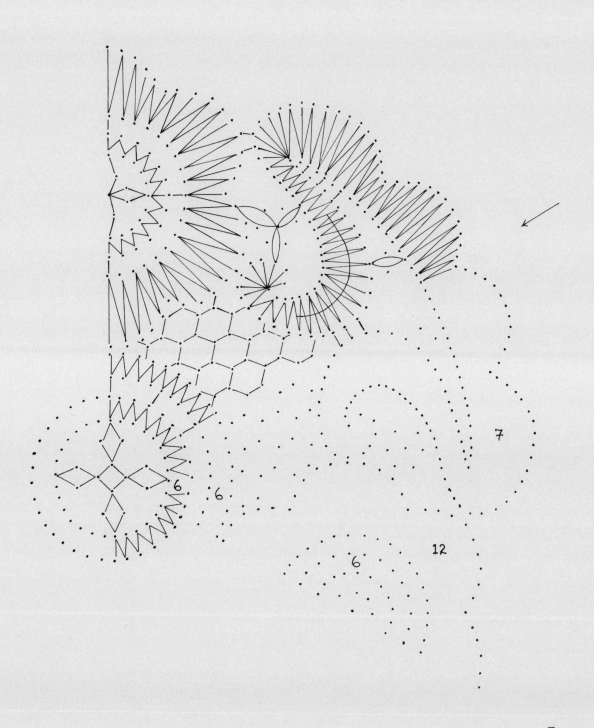

6

6

7

6

12

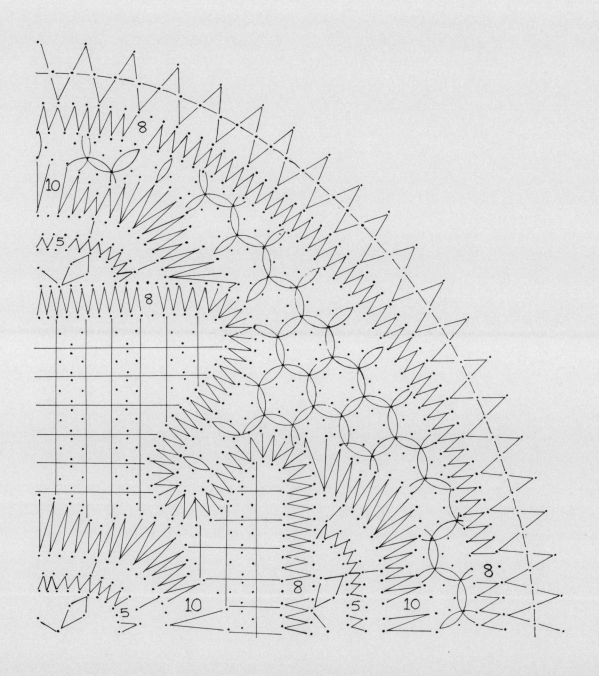

22